Pocket Apocalypse

Pocket Apocalypse

Katarzyna Borun-Jagodzinska

translated from the Polish by
Gerry Murphy

intermediate translator
Karolina Barski

SOUTHWORDeditions

First published in 2005
by Southword Editions,
the Munster Literature Centre,
Frank O'Connor House, 84 Douglas Street,
Cork, Ireland.

Set in Centaur
Printed in Ireland by Colour Books, Dublin.

ISBN: I-905002-II-4
www.munsterlit.ie

This book is the ninth in a series of thirteen published as
part of the official programme for Cork 2005: European
Capital of Culture

Cork 2005

European Capital of Culture

Acknowledgements

Cover Image: *Gold Feathers and Wine* by Paul La Rocque
monoprint 86 x 76 cm

Contents

Untitled
(for A.B.)

In catastrophes
our letters are lost,
as if the postman
could save us…

In a dark room
tenderness yellows with age —
the very letters you carried out
of the burning refinery.

The Last Resort

"On the other side there is nothing"
said the old hag,
dragging herself into the poem.
Although if it was anyone else,
especially an acquaintance,
we would never be quite so blunt.

"On the other side there is nothing"
she reiterated.
A wind blew cold and empty (from the other side?)
as we shivered
in the tar-melting heat.
All this about nothing (not even another side)
as we slipped past
the last stop.

Othello's First Book

Which came first?
The bitter seed or the shadowy tree?
Bitterness can prepare the way for sweetness,
though the tart seed permeates the apple.
A green-eyed monster already awake,
a worm turning just under the skin.
Love creeps past on tiptoes
so as not to arouse the beast.

Gothic Tale

So quiet here at dawn,
no one remembers
the squinting window
in the clock face.
So quiet,
even though the clock's
relentless hands
decapitate
over-ardent lovers
and the trees creak
under the increasing weight
of the sky.

In the Convent Courtyard

All things rest easy
in your hands Lord.
Still, I am not a moth
and You are not an idle boy,
casually stripping my wings.
Surely this familiar gloom
that gathers around me
is the after-shadow
of your smile.

Theresa at the Laundry

(for Jan Sochon)

Those, for whom they smooth out
      for whom they smooth out
      for whom they straighten out.

Those, for whom they even out
      for whom they even out,
      for whom they erase
      the smallest stain,
      burn the mattresses,
      sweep the cells,
      sterilize with boiling water
      every physical trace,
      so that later
      they can retouch the eyelashes,
      renew the face-paint,
      because I did not seem
      quite dead enough.

Those, I will never forgive.

What's more, I intend to out-pray
that blue-rinsed sky
and those paper roses.

Family Album

Here is a photograph of my father,
to his left my sisters.
Maybe I should leave this
for another occasion,
am I asking too much?

In the photograph,
I am right beside my father.
Almost as if I was trying
to hide him in my shadow.
Too late, how could I have forgotten
Job's outrageous fate.

Photograph of Theresa Martin as Joan of Arc

Here, I am a small Joan,
well, obviously a little older.
In this ferocious tableau:
full armour, spear, sword, shield,
grin glinting like polished steel —
there is no inkling
that I am slowly climbing
the smouldering pyre of my own body.
The body in the context of martyrdom,
nothing else.
I'm still waiting
on a sign from Heaven,
although I have a good idea
about the mechanics of disintegration
and the indestructible lumps of ore
they will recover from my ashes.

Snapshot

Theresa looks down
and laughs out loud:
"oh my little thimbles
filled to the brim".
The child
smiles up at her,
as if Theresa
had conjured them
and herself
out of thin air.

Theology

If you are already There
then listen,
listen to our requests.
Put in a good word
since you are near
the seat of all powers.

And even if?
Even if you are already asleep
like all mortals
on the way to Judgement Day,
He knows, even if you never will,
so stop asking.

Shut up and listen,
just listen.

Pocket Apocalypse
(for Piotr Bratkowski)

This is what
it might look like:
blizzards,
darkness,
fallen power lines
and a telephone
that comes to life
only to announce
your own death.

Tower

We will raise it.
Speaking with one voice,
we will prolong the moment
of clarity
before the inevitable
clamour of tongues.
We will climb
higher and higher,
lighter than cigarette smoke
into the deafening silence.

Van Morrison Plays Mother Goose

How many miles to Babylon?
We will return before the fire dies out.
Babylon has smooth straight roads,
a tower in which a frantic glass elevator
races up and down,
lanterns that blaze out intermittently
for no discernible reason.
How many miles to Babylon?
I press a single cotton thread
into a small ball of wax.
How many miles to Babylon?
I light the candle at both ends
and apply a blow-torch to the middle.
We will return before the fire dies out.

Love's Young Dream

The young poet sings:
"I only exist to love myself and nobody else"
As he touched himself
his skin shrivelled
and became brown
as if burnt in an oven.
Suddenly his body
was the body
of a dead, long barren woman.
The old poet gazed through the window
at a beautiful boy.

That's Women For You...
(for Tad Komendant)

The poet's habitual curses
break over their marble heads.
His blasphemous rants
dwindling to mad whimpers.
Who will judge him?
Certainly not women.
Even if they endure,
it will be only to bathe
and clothe his dead body.

Tosca

Art is no way to live,
yet so many scrounge a living from it.
Receptions, anniversaries, charity balls,
concerts at dawn, noon, evening and midnight.
Singing is no career for a dignified woman.
For orphans I sing slow consumptive arias,
for the Chief of Police I play the dying waif.
No career for an honest woman,
probably not,
yet is a career in the police
suitable for an ardent lover,
or the life of the poet
the best grounding for a patriot?
As usual it's all on my shoulders.
I usher in each revolution
with a high C on my lips.
It's me you hear, only me.

Scarpia

"It won't do madam,
your voice is breaking
and today is the premiere"
She pretended not to hear.
She imagined the smear on the window
was an eye.
More like the blood stain
of a lover I had only finished interrogating.
He denied everything, as I knew he would.
I knew she would do anything
to save him, so I pretended she could.
Actually I detest shameless women,
even as she undid the first button,
she could see me placing the signed death warrant
in the drawer.

Mimi's Aria

I cook for myself,
still my hands are cold.
Once again the spoon rattles
in the empty pot.
The oven no longer heats,
the last chair has gone for kindling.
I sit on the floor.
When someone comes in
I pretend that I have lost the keys
to the recently stocked larder.
I have no illusions that anyone
would wish to paint my scrawny hips,
not to mention my gaunt face.
Neither will they describe me
in a poem.
The poets died out long ago,
too much fat around their stony hearts.
It's miserable here, sitting on the floor.
In the flat below,
the neighbours children
are playing suicide bomber.

Fidelio I

Why can't I change my skin,
even for a moment,
especially when she smells
of perfume and tears?
It's not as easy
as you think,
tearing my eyes from her
like a bandage
from an open wound,
from her parted lips,
pouting with regret.
I know how this would end
if I were a man.
I also know,
that if I were a man,
I would be a short, thin man,
with a sharp nose and utterly bald.
So forget I mentioned it.

Fidelio II

How I long to escort you,
dressed as a man,
from this prison,
where they lengthen your sentence
every month.
Dressed as a man,
because in any other garb
we would not be allowed
to even mention freedom.
How I long to escort you
to a safe place,
safe but wide-open.
Where our thoughts
would not over-burden us,
where our bodies would no longer
be seen as an open wound.
There we would have our own names
and the word "woman" would never mean
a swift kick in the teeth.

Aida

The last stroke of the trowel
and we are walled-up.
Very little air to breathe,
not to mind sing.
And yet we sing,
although what they expected
were loving whispers
and desperate notes
written in blood
on scraps of paper.
We sing.
Outside the army draws near,
bullets smash holes
in the plaster
spattering our faces.
Yet neither one of us squeals.

Scarpia's Aria

I also have a heart,
though you mightn't believe it.
A certain woman told me:
"Before dawn my daughter seduced the executioner,
it didn't work, he used her, then hurried off
to lather the noose."
"Later he sent me the soap, still marked by the rope,
so that I could clean my son's corpse."
"I thanked him, one must be grateful for any mercy."
I pity my inferiors, I pity everybody.

Apollo

The last time the gods
were among us,
we danced 'till dawn.
We made love,
we tore down the darkness
with our bare hands,
we blinked away the shadows.
We cursed mere males,
praised real men.
The last time the gods
were among us.

And now,
touching ourselves,
we rail at nature
and the gods who lied.

We gave away our dreams, our time.
We kept nothing for ourselves,
not even our secrets.

With you we never win,
in your merciless light
we hang like grotesque fruit,
waiting for you to cut us down.

Cocoon

With God you have no downfalls,
in God you can disappear.

You can bury yourself
as in an avalanche,
surviving beneath tons of snow.

Breathing in your vaulted grotto,
snug in your glistening igloo.

The mist
unravels the thread of itself
into the sky.

Thread of
returning snow.

Chrysalis
for thread,
chrysalis
for nothing.

You will peek out
only to see frozen silk.

You will see nothing
only fluttering snow.

Aurora

As for these skies,
hanging in curtains and coils,
folds of glitter
and a red blizzard.

As for this earth
and its constant embrace,
its warm hands upon us
as upon sleeping children.

As for this water,
its persistent hiss
chasing us up
the highest tower.

As for this air,
it lifts us up,
blows us about,
dries us off,
until we are drenched again.

Nothing is certain:
the sky clouds over,
the rain rinses us
from the earth.

God Bless Iowa City

No love,
nor belief,
nor death.

Only cholesterol-free,
musically treated optimism
in an air-tight tube.

No belief,
nor love,
nor death.

Only riders,
gales,
dawn stretched
along the edge of the highway
like a squashed skunk.

America:
An electronic alarm clock
with its terrible inscription:
"Everyone harms, the last kills"

City Poets

It would be easier for us
if we stopped saying it straight,
if we hid our meaning in metaphor,
if we dealt solely in obscurity.
The city sells itself over and over
for false friendships, for temporary gain.
Look at the previous dwellers
abandoned outside its gates,
dumped in its overflowing cemeteries.
We are no different,
our home is a dark stain
on a tablecloth,
a heart fashioned inexpertly
on a sewing machine.
We are foundlings
left in boxes outside orphanages,
squirming and wailing without end.

A Civic Lyric

When you arrive,
please take your shoes off
at the doorstep and enter slowly.
I want to take you in
like a newly discovered city;
run through abandoned gardens,
rest in the dappled shade
of over-arching trees,
take shelter in derelict churches,
wander through sunlit alleyways,
suffer the soft buffeting of numberless ghosts,
throw wads of cash into silent fountains
and return again and again and again...

The Forest

It still terrifies us,
every murmur in its black depths,
the sudden flight of a startled bird
making us dive for cover.
The city groans
with its own metallic voice,
yet we have tamed it.
Still, one false move,
one unfamiliar fragrance
lingered over
and the beast
will tear out our throats.

The Garden

Someone was still calling:
"Nanny, Nanny, Nanny…"
Grubby fingernails were inspected,
ears checked for wax,
fingers for chilblains.
One letter after another
was being forced into demands:
"Don't touch, don't litter, don't cheat,
at least for granny's sake."
Uneaten dinners are getting cold,
little fingers are sticking
to the pages of forbidden books.
The smell of tears floats in on the after-dinner silence,
once again someone has grown old
in the children's garden.

Evenings Closing in

Shadows deepen quickly,
a path on the green grows sharper,
until the green slips into darkness,
the blood surges with sudden effervescence
yeast dances just under the skin.
Children drink blue air
from their mothers' lips.
Grandmothers buy salt,
throwing it over their left shoulders
as they walk,
so that any lost travellers
will find their way back
to their discarded bodies.

Night

Something wakes me,
the sound of a heavy bundle
being thrown down a chute,
a swift, fatal fall.

Perhaps it was
only some old books,
or maybe some drowned kittens,
or a baby wrapped in newspaper,
or even a corpse cut into manageable chunks…
Maybe, maybe not,
trouble is we don't have a chute.

On Tiptoes

Quieter
than the breath of a sleeping child.
Don't try to name
the unspeakable shadow
which slipped under the wall
and vanished.
It was trailing blood downstairs
with a soother in its mouth
and a stiletto in its hand.

Escape

We pitched our tent beside the road.
This would be our life:
Ash, oak and a few scraggy plants
the developers overlooked.
A life discovered
like a hoofprint
on a country road
and preserved in ice
in a bucket in the hallway.
A life of wilderness views
filling every window,
where the night sky
is dizzy with stars,
echoing with barking dogs,
whispering with the idolatrous prayers
of the cat to the swallow.

A friend, tasting our organic jams,
at our plain wooden table says:
"rustic arts are the new wave".
We play dumb.
Beyond the darkened window,
beyond the reach of calloused hands,
the city howls on its leash.

Something is Happening in Belgium

Not that you could tell:
Suburbs, gardens, solid brick homes.
A professional soldier
finds the Muse
for a tantalizing moment
and leaves his wife
and two growing daughters.
Since then he occasionally visits
an old neighbour for a beer.
And noticing his quizzical look asks:
"What, pray tell, would I do now
with three unforgiving women?"

Tenant

The big boy has lost it.
He wears striped stockings with silver threads.
"Kiss me hard" he says and holds out his hand.
He has soft skin and rippling muscles.
Love knows no boundaries.
"You're soft" says the hard bed.
"You're good" says the white wall.
"You're faithful" says the keyhole.
"I like your kisses" says an old teacup,
everything within the four walls
declares its undying devotion.
The boy cleans the rooms,
the rooms wipe the dust from his eyes.
The house embraces him
with frightening intensity.
The big boy has lost it.
He will not leave the house.

Ballad Without a Moral

She has gone back to her meadows,
that little bitch with the innocent look.
Thorns prick her soles,
rocks stub her toes.
Her bandit lover waits
by the city with her stolen heart.
He cuts lengths of string for luck.
He counts his ill-gotten gains,
pieces of eight, emeralds, rubies,
he dumps the rest.

At the roadside Inn,
a sullen tart refills the glasses.
The braided, fair haired bitch
chokes on cheap wine,
sprawled across the table,
squeezing in her sweaty palm
a short piece of string

Poland 1981

Maybe she was a dream,
maybe she did'nt exist,
though everyone racked their brains
trying to remember her–
she lived, loved, suffered,
she sang between the lines
in hundreds of poems
born from her ashes.
She is a word worn thin
by tenderness,
eaten through by terrible family histories:
the son did not return from battle,
the daughter sold herself
for a bowl of soup,
the first cousin picks through rubbish
in Berlin.
Father and mother wait in vain
for their return.
And every year
the winter gets longer and longer.

Séance

We decided to call up the dead,
to summon the spirits of the celebrated departed:
Statesmen, poets and saints.
Someone was tapping gently
on the window, a plate shifted slightly
towards the letter "c",
a long low moan, then silence.
Reluctantly, we rose from the table.
Then they came,
shyly with lowered heads,
staying close to the door.
The medium stood at the door,
stroking their bowed heads,
reassuring them, forgiving them

Song of Desire

I don't want to have you,
I don't want to harm you,
I don't want to kill you,
at least not quite yet.
My lips remain tightly pursed,
my hands retain their icy clutch.
Yet I have only to glance at you
to raise a prickle of heat
on your skin

Song for a New House

May you have as much luck
as the length of a piece of string;
as much warmth
as you have coal in your bunker;
as much light as you have windows;
as many enemies as you can count.

May you have a heart
like the one you were born with;
as much taste as a squeeze of lemon
on your lips;
as much freedom
as your cell allows;
as much hope as you can inflate.

May you have as much room
as you can swing a cat;
meadows as wide
as you can see with one eye.
May you be your own judge,
your own ruthless executioner.

Solo Song

Footsteps
and an open book,
as if someone interrupted
your reading for a moment.
Footsteps
and a torn sheet,
the field beneath the snow
cut up by sleighs.
Footsteps
and whispers on the stairs,
but no one knocks,
no one says "may I".
And so,
water drips from the tap,
cheese patiently ferments
under the lampshade,
and so on.

Gabriel

I can't, I just can't.
My father is too old,
it would kill my mother.
I can't, I mean it, I can't.
As for my brothers,
they would kill me,
not to mention the neighbours,
they would kill us all.
Just leave it, I can't.

He went two doors down.
The windows lit up
as if for a wedding.
I was left with cold mountain air
pouring in under the door
and a sudden blizzard
swirling through the house.

The Last Photograph

Before someone comes
with the flash and the pan,
before they set up the camera,
you will stomp out the silence
and speak in whispers.
You will stomp out the silence
and speak in whispers,
as if you were afraid
of frightening the Angel of Death.
Don't worry, he fears nothing,
not even his own shadow.

Medea's Dry Eyes

Only onions and smoke
prick a reluctant tear.
A grain of salt
melts on a dead eyeball.
Nothing left behind
in reparation-
a younger brother's
severed finger
wrapped in a note
in the pocket of a housecoat:
"Don't wait any longer,
just go…"

Manifesto for My Friends

Before you die,
before you grow up,
before you get sucked in by the city
through the cracks in the pavement.
Before you snuff it,
before you develop a passion
for elevator doors
and a wife held hostage
in an mineshaft
by adolescent terrorists,
among which you recognise
your eldest daughter.
Before you shuffle off,
before you give up
waiting for that perfect moment,
when truth will sing
from the same hymn-sheet as lies,
before you decide not to publish
fragments of our conversations
in your best-selling autobiography,
before you decline to answer
any questions on local radio
leading to eloquent silence.
Before you step
over to the other side,
convince us once more
that those distant traffic lights
are actually drops of blood
falling into the grass.

Little Lord English

Lord English strolls across a frozen meadow.
What of the letters nobody sent,
stillborn in their envelopes.
Lord English firmly believes
in the Queen and the Royal Mail,
in the vigorous use of the cane,
in the imperial tilt of his snout.
In the playground,
using the tip of his umbrella,
he writes mildly pornographic words
in a child's scrawl.
Only thirty, he is already
his own desert island.
Lord English strolls across a frozen meadow,
through a blizzard of unwritten letters.

Marlow Poet

A thin poet
is struggling to keep a fat detective
within his scrawny frame.
Just look at the fag-end
stuck to his bored lower lip.
The poet has his own Sunset Boulevard:
cheap cafes, where the lonely crowds
are rented from Hopper.
Where intellectuals are no less willing
than millionaires' wives,
where unused metaphors
can become a shot in the knee,
or a kick in the arse.
Marlow is a private poet.
A thin poet loves a fat detective,
the fat detective cannot abide poets.
Marlow smiles the weary smile
of a ginger tomcat

The Match

There were many of them
and each one had a quadrupled shadow.
One shadow remembered its first cigarette,
the second its first swig of vodka,
the third its first love,
the fourth its first encounter with death.
There were many of them
and each one made up
one arm of a cross.
The first arm remembered
the taste of nausea from the smoke,
the second the burning acid in the throat,
the third the sweat of a woman,
the fourth the sickly-sweet scent
of a corpse.
There were many of them, too many of them
and each had a quadrupled shadow.
The quadrupled shadow
laid itself down in the grass
and gave itself up to the floodlights.

Is That It?

We no longer fear the loss of the world,
as opposed to our elders.
We know,
we know with certainty
that it will endure,
rolled up like a tent,
to be pitched for one night
beside the road to nowhere.
Let's promise each other,
that we will hold each other tightly
against all possibilities.
It'll be alright,
everything will be all right